levers

Levers

Chris Ollerenshaw and Pat Triggs
Photographs by Peter J Millard

Contents

A & C Black · London

What's in the toybox?

Does your toybox get in a mess? Some of
the toys in this toybox have been tidied
away into tins. But the lid of one tin is
stuck. How would you get it open? Fingers
are not strong enough on their own.

A spoon
could be
useful.

What's inside this blue tin? It looks like a muddle. But all these things belong together, and they belong with the spoon. There is a way in which they are all alike.

Look at the red and yellow signal. Look back at the spoon. Is the movement of the signal like the movement of the spoon opening the tin? The arm of the signal wouldn't have been much use in helping to get the tin open. But picture in your mind the signal on its post and the spoon against the tin.

The arm of the signal moving up and down and the spoon lifting the lid of the tin are both LEVERS. All the things in the tin have something to do with levers.

How does a spoon become a lever?

A spoon is a tool designed for spooning up things like soup and cornflakes and custard. But there are things about the shape of a spoon that can make it a useful lever.

When you put one end of the spoon under the lid and push down on the other end to open the tin, the spoon is working like a lever. Look carefully. Can you see where the spoon is balancing on the edge of the tin? When you push down on one end of the spoon the other end goes up, just like a seesaw, and pushes off the lid.

The place where the spoon is balancing is called a PIVOT. All levers have a pivot.

4

Collect some levers like these and discover what working with levers feels like. Try doing some levering. Notice where the pivot is each time you try a different lever. Could you make a lever to help you lift something like a pile of books? What would you need?

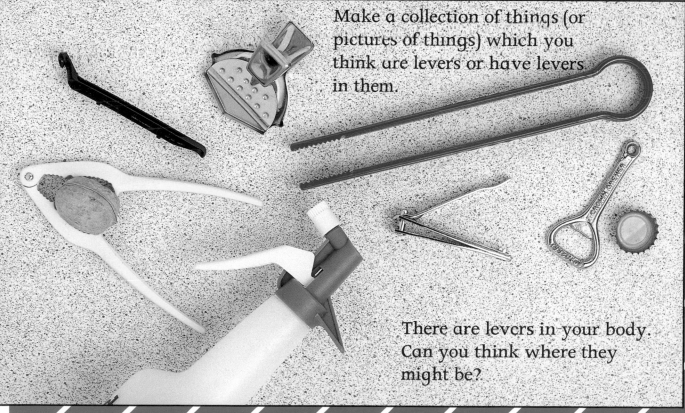

Make a collection of things (or pictures of things) which you think are levers or have levers in them.

There are levers in your body. Can you think where they might be?

Body levers

Every time you eat some food or walk across a room you are using the levers in your body. Arms, legs, jaw ... all these parts of your skeleton contain levers. The pivot is the hinged joint which allows the bones to swivel but keeps them together. When a lever pivots its two parts must stay together for it to work.

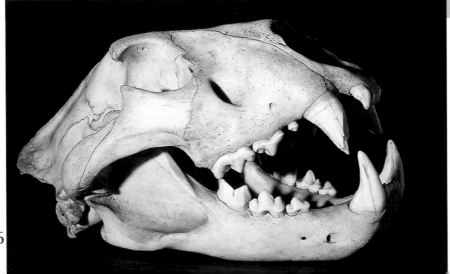

Humans are born with lots of useful pivots in their bodies and so are other animals. Look at this jaw bone of a lion. Can you see how the bones are hinged together?

Thousands of years ago, people began to see how the same kind of lever movement that makes a hinge could be useful to them in their everyday lives. Look at this hinged lid of a purse. It is nearly 1300 years old.

We still use hinges in lots of ways. How many things can you find around your home that have hinges that help them to work? What would we do without them?

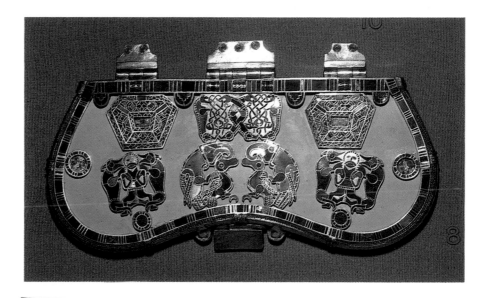

Why are levers useful?

A lever is a machine that helps us to do things. When we talk about machines we usually think of complicated things like computers and racing cars. But when you used the spoon as a lever it became a simple machine doing a job.

Here are some other simple machines that work as levers. Think about what they do.

Levers make different kinds of work easier. When you are not strong enough to do some things a lever can help you. It doesn't make you stronger, but it uses the strength you have and makes it work more effectively so the job is easier.

But that's not all levers can do.

You can find out what other uses levers have by making some yourself. You will need: a piece of thick board, some strips of thin card (you could use cereal box card), drawing pins, paper fasteners.

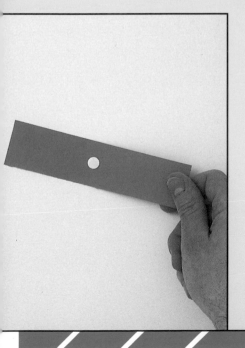

Pin one strip of card to the board. Move one end of the strip with your hand. Does the pin allow you to move the strip up and down? If it does, the pin is a pivot and you have made a lever!

Notice how the ends of the strip are moving. If you make one end of a lever go down, the other end goes up. If you make one end go up, the other end goes down.

That's one important thing to know about levers if you want to make things work.

Try moving the pin to different positions on the strip. What difference does it make?

Making levers

Now try adding a second strip like the blue one in the picture. Make a hole in both pieces of card where you want the join to be and use a paper fastener to hold them together.

Try moving the end of the strip you have added. Watch how it moves. Watch how the first strip moves. You have made two levers.

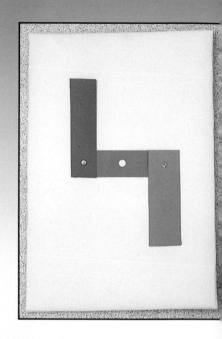

Now add a third strip like this green one. Try the movement again. How many levers have you made now?

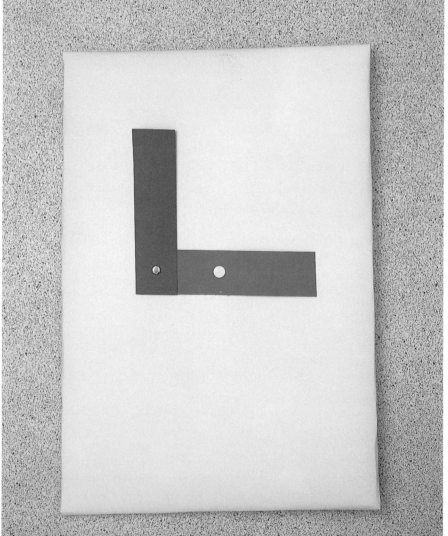

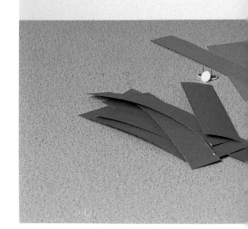

To find out, how many levers you have made, look carefully at the green strip that you have just added. Is it swivelling on the paper fastener? You can check whether it is by looking at the ends of the strips. If your third strip is not pivoting on the paper fastener, it will only be able to move in the same direction as the end of the strip which is pinned to the board.

If the green strip isn't able to swivel around, the paper fastener is not a pivot and you haven't made a third lever.

On the green strip in the picture, the fastener is not a pivot. There are still only two levers.

Can you think how you could make the green strip into a lever?

Changing direction

Before you can turn the green strip into a lever, you have to find a way of controlling how that strip moves. Put some mapping pins along each side of your strip. (Make sure you don't pin the strip down so that it can't move at all!)

Now move your blue lever up and down. Watch your green strip. It has to move in the pathway made by the pins and to do that it has to pivot on the paper fastener. When it does that, you'll have three levers all moving in different directions.

Look carefully at HOW the levers are moving. When you pull the blue lever down what does the green one do? What happens when you push the blue lever up? Use guide pins to make different pathways for the green strip. What happens? Do all the pathways work equally well?

Here's a challenge. How many strips can you link together to make a sequence of levers? Try using longer or shorter strips. Use guide pins if you think they will help. Remember to check whether each strip is a new lever when you count to find your total.

Here's a pop-up toy. You can't see how it works but you now know enough about levers to work it out. Try to make a drawing of the movement.

You could use your lever arrangements to design your own pop-up toy.

13

Turning small movements into bigger ones

This toy signal uses a lever. You can see the pivot that keeps the post and the signal arm together and allows you to move the arm. Use two strips and your board to make a lever that works like the signal.

It's not a complicated movement, but it will show you something about levers that makes them useful.

With your fingers near the pivot fastener move the signal arm up and down. Notice how you only have to move the pivot end of the arm a little way to make its other end move over a much bigger distance.

What happens if you put short, middle-sized and long strips on the same pivot? When you move the pivot end, how far does each lever move? What would you have to do to make a lever that would move even further?

The designer of this machine for enlarging drawings knew that levers can turn small movements into bigger ones. As one pencil traces the small drawing, the other pencil makes an exact copy, but in a larger size. Levers in machines like this one can help you to do things that you couldn't do by yourself.

Making things move

Here's a different toy signal. You can move the signal arm without touching it. Can you see how it works? Its levers are linked together in a sequence.

Make a picture on your board to show how the levers work together to move the signal arm.

If you are not sure whether a pin or fastener in your picture is a pivot, try taking it away. Does your signal still work? If it doesn't, you have removed a pivot and broken the chain of levers.

This pedal bin is a lid-lifting machine that works in almost exactly the same way as the signalling machine. Use your pins, fasteners and strips to show how it works on your board. You will not have to change the picture much. How could you show that when the pedal goes down, the lid goes up?

If you change your strip picture around a bit you can show how this chicken pecking toy works. The signal, the pedal bin and the chicken toy all have the same number of levers which work together in a very similar way.

Making work easier

What have you found out about levers so far? Levers help you put more force on things that are hard to move or lift. They can make something move in a different direction.
And they can turn a small movement into a larger one.

We can use what we know about levers to design machines to do things we can't do. You can put together two or more of the things that levers can do to make something work.

Look at this toy. When you pull down on the string its arms and legs move in different directions. You have to pull down only a little way to make the toy's hands and feet move a long way.

Can you work out what is happening at the back of this toy? Where do you think the pivots are on each lever? What job is the string doing? How is it attached? Try making a model of the movement using your board and strips. Could you use a card lever instead of string?

You could try designing another toy that works like this one.

Keeping the balance

Six thousand years ago, people used their knowledge that levers can be balanced to invent a machine for weighing things. They hung a beam from a cord making sure there was a central pivot. The Romans used this idea to make a machine called a steelyard.

Can you see the steelyard on the right of this picture? The meat to be weighed was put into the pan. The weight on the left of the machine was moved along the arm until it balanced with the pan. The weight of the meat was shown by how far the weight had to be moved along the arm.

Doctors today use a weighing machine with a steelyard lever movement. Perhaps there is one in the medical room at your school?

Makers of mobiles and moving sculptures like this one have to find the point of balance of the levers to make their designs work.

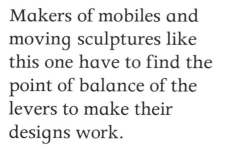

You could try designing a mobile like this one.
You will need:
some wire
some thread
some different-sized things to hang from the mobile e.g. conkers, buttons.

How will you make it work? Think about the distance of each object from the pivot to help you make everything balance.

Making the difference

The distance from the pivot is also important when you are using levers to move things. Sometimes you can open the lid of a tin with a coin. Sometimes a coin doesn't work and you have to use a spoon. Sometimes the lid is stuck so hard a spoon doesn't work and you have to use something like a screwdriver.

Your hand is pushing with the same force on the coin, the spoon and the screwdriver. The lever is making the difference. Can you work out what is happening?

What is it about the screwdriver that makes it better than the coin for opening a very stuck lid? Why is the screwdriver better than the coin at making the force of your hand strong enough to lift the lid?

Naming the parts

When you are opening a tin, the force of your hand is one part of the lever movement. At one end of every lever there has to be some kind of force or effort. You don't always have to feel as if you are pushing or pulling – when you sit on a seesaw a pulling down force is in action.

Load is the word to describe whatever is going to be moved by the lever. Sometimes if it's something heavy it really looks like a load. But sometimes you can't really see the load and it doesn't look heavy.

In all lever movements there has to be:
A LOAD to be moved.
A PIVOT to make the difference.
An EFFORT to be made.

Can you point to the load, the pivot and the effort in this picture? (Hint: the pivot is in between the effort and the load in this lever movement.)

Look at this trolley. This time, the load is between the effort and the pivot.

Can you point to the load, the effort and the pivot in this lever movement?

Did you notice that the load and the pivot are closer together than the effort and the pivot? Can you think why this is? (Hint: remember what you found out about the distance from the pivot.)

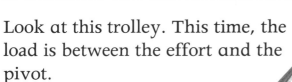

If you put two levers together you can make really useful machines like these. How do these levers work? Can you see the effort, the load and the pivot? Do they follow the same pattern in each movement?

25

All sorts of uses

There's another thing that levers can do which makes them very useful in the design of all kinds of machines. Try this out on your board. Cut a circle of card. Attach a strip lever to the circle with a fastener. Pin the circle to the board. Move your lever up and down in a straight line. Can you see how your straight line movement turns the card disc in a circular movement?

Being able to turn up and down movement into circular movement is very useful for all kinds of machines. Over 200 years ago, James Watt invented a machine which turned up and down movement into circular movement. The machine provided the power for many other machines in factories.

Using levers also allows us to fold things into a smaller space. Look for the pivots or hinges on some foldaway things like these that you may find at home or in school. Can you see how they work?

Make a moving picture

Every day we use machines which are designed by people who have found out what levers can do. Often we don't know we are using levers. Remember that we use levers when we are eating or walking.

People who design and make pop-up books are called paper engineers. They use levers to design the movements in their pop-up books.

You can make your own moving picture like this one by using the blueprint on pages 30 and 31.

The cat is hiding in the flowering bush. The bird sits in the grass between the bushes. The cat pounces! Too late! The bird has flown into the other bush.

These pictures show what happens to the bird and the cat. You will have learned enough to design your own levers to make them appear and disappear. The blueprint will show you how to make the model itself.

Index

This paperback edition published 1999 by
A & C Black (Publishers) Limited
35 Bedford Row, London, WC1R 4JH.

First published in hardback 1991.

Text © 1991 Chris Ollerenshaw and Pat Triggs
All photographs © Peter J Millard except
pg 6 John Heinrich; pg 7 CM Dixon;
pg 8 Emrhys Barrell; pg 20 CM Dixon;
pg 21 Pat Triggs.

ISBN 0-7136-5230-6

Model and blueprint by David Ollerenshaw
Illustrations by Dennis Tinkler.
Designed by Michael Leaman.

A CIP catalogue record for this book
is available from the British Library.

Filmset by August Filmsetting, Haydock, St Helens.
Printed in Belgium by Proost International Book
Production.

Acknowledgments

The photographer, authors and publishers would
like to thank the following people whose help and
co-operation made this book possible: Juliette,
Charlene, Beini, Rosie, Ahmet, Ryan, David and
Tony and the staff and pupils at Avondale Park
Primary School, Royal Borough of Kensington
and Chelsea.

Pouncing Cat

The cat is hiding in the flowering bush. The bird sits in the grass between the bushes. The cat pounces! Too late! The bird has flown into the other bush.

Make this little story happen. Trace these plans onto card, using corrugated cardboard for the shed cutout. See how they all fit together but don't glue yet.

Work out your levers in the space below the shed. The animals should be moved using a lever sticking out of an end wall. Make the cat pounce DOWN and the bird fly UP. Leave glueing until the end.

TREE SUPPORTS keep the trees upright. Trace onto card, cut and glue into place, matching the letters. Shorten th if you need

Glue tab A | TREE SUPPORT

Glue tab B | TREE SUPPORT

Glue tab C   Glue tab C

Fold this tab forwards before glueing.

F

G

Glue tab A

Glue tab C here.   Trees should stand on this line.   Glue tab C

This is a lawn. Can you make it look like one?

E

D

30

TRACE these shapes onto card. Trace the left side of the blueprint first. Next, position one vertical blue line on top of the other. Then continue tracing. Use corrugated cardboard for the shed cutout.

CUT along all solid black lines.

FOLD along all dotted black lines (score along dotted lines with an electrical screwdriver before folding).

GREEN lines show where to glue. **RED** lines give ideas for decoration.

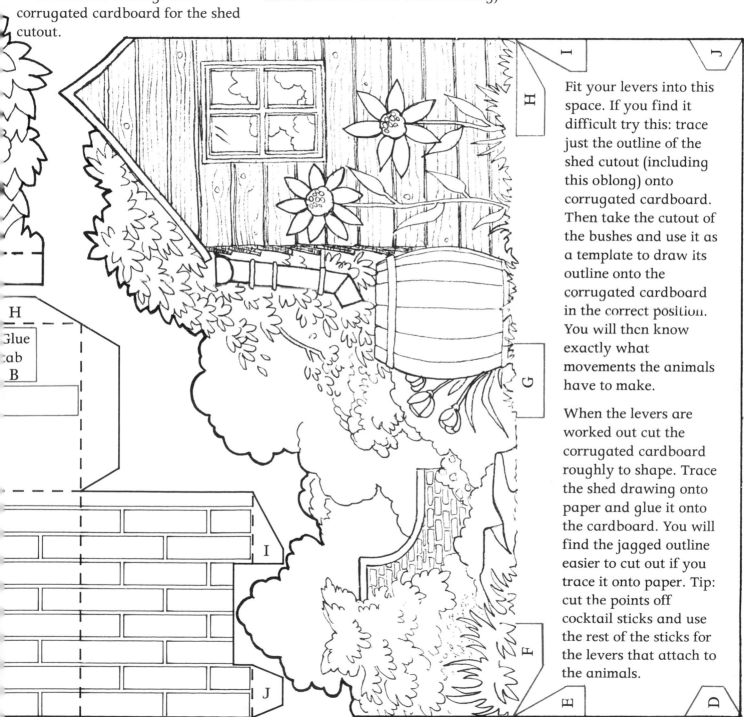

Fit your levers into this space. If you find it difficult try this: trace just the outline of the shed cutout (including this oblong) onto corrugated cardboard. Then take the cutout of the bushes and use it as a template to draw its outline onto the corrugated cardboard in the correct position. You will then know exactly what movements the animals have to make.

When the levers are worked out cut the corrugated cardboard roughly to shape. Trace the shed drawing onto paper and glue it onto the cardboard. You will find the jagged outline easier to cut out if you trace it onto paper. Tip: cut the points off cocktail sticks and use the rest of the sticks for the levers that attach to the animals.

31

Notes for teachers and parents

Each title in this series promotes investigation as a way of learning about science and being scientific. Children are invited to try things out and think things through for themselves. It's very important for the children to handle the materials mentioned in the books, as only by making their own scientific explorations can they construct an explanation that works for them.

Each Toybox Science book is structured so that it follows a planned cycle of learning. At the **orientation** stage, children draw on their previous experience to organise their ideas. **Exploration** encourages clarification and refining of ideas and leads to **investigation**. At this stage children are testing and comparing, a process which leads to developing, restructuring and replacing ideas. **Reviewing** can occur at the end or throughout as appropriate. Children discuss what they have found out and draw conclusions, perhaps using recorded data. Finally, open-ended problems provide opportunities for **application** of acquired knowledge and skills.

In writing these books we drew on our practical experience of this cycle to select and sequence activities, to frame questions, to make strategic decisions about when to introduce information and specialized vocabulary, when to summarise and suggest recording. The use of industrial applications and the introduction of a historical perspective are to encourage the linkage of ideas.

The **blueprint** at the end of each book encourages children to apply their learning in a new situation. There is no 'right' answer to how to get the inside mechanism to work; the problem could be solved in any number of ways and children should be left to find their own.

The national curriculum: the first four books in the series are concerned with energy, forces and the nature of materials explored within an overall notion of movement and how things work.

LEVERS

Levers occur in many contexts, some more obvious than others. All levers have a pivot (fulcrum). Levers make work easier by controlling movement (kinetic) energy and are often found working together with gears.

Examples in the book demonstrate that levers enable a smaller movement to be converted into a larger one (p. 14 signal arm, pp. 18/19, moving model frog); are used to increase the force applied to lift and move a mass (p. 25 trolley, p. 4 opening a tin); are used to fold things away (p. 27 clothes horse, glasses). Body levers are shown to be an important part of movement in animals.

The work with card strips allows for the development of ideas about controlling movement but they are most effective and understood best when *preceded* by the first hand experience of using a wide variety of levers. Ideas can be consolidated and developed by applying lever principles in further exploration and by identifying levers in many other situations.

Resources

Children working with this book will be best supported by:

- A collection of assorted materials similar to those mentioned in the book.
- A resource box of tools and basics like paper fasteners, rubber bands, etc and everyday junk materials (to be stored and labelled to allow children to access them independently).
- The availability of construction kits.
- Collections of toys and real world objects similar to those mentioned in the book.
- Books and pictures related to the topic of the book to support enquiry and investigation.
- Visits to places where they can see industrial applications, current and historical.